Prepare to Quit

Finding the Keys to a Spirit-Filled Life
Beyond Alcohol

Rose Ann Forte

Copyright © 2025, Rose Ann Forte

All rights reserved. No part of this book may be used or reproduced by any means, graphic, electronic, or mechanical (including any information storage retrieval system) without the express written permission from the author, except in the case of brief quotations for use in articles and reviews wherein appropriate attribution of the source is made.

Publishing support provided by
Ignite Press
55 Shaw Ave. Suite 204
Clovis, CA 93612
www.IgnitePress.us

ISBN: 979-8-9866084-3-3
ISBN: 979-8-9866084-4-0 (E-book)

For bulk purchases and for booking, contact:
Rose Ann Forte
roseann@choosefreedom.today
www.choosefreedom.today

Because of the dynamic nature of the Internet, web addresses or links contained in this book may have been changed since publication and may no longer be valid. The content of this book and all expressed opinions are those of the author and do not reflect the publisher or the publishing team. The author is solely responsible for all content included herein.

Unless otherwise indicated, Scripture quotations taken from the Holy Bible, New Living Translation (NLT). Copyright ©1996, 2004, 2007 by Tyndale House Foundation. Used by permission of Tyndale House Publishers, Inc.

Unless otherwise indicated, Scripture quotations taken from the Holy Bible, New International Version (NIV). Copyright © 1973, 1978, 1984, 2011 by Biblica, Inc.™. Used by permission. All rights reserved.

Unless otherwise indicated, Scripture quotations taken from the English Standard Version (ESV). Copyright © 2001 by Crossway, a publishing ministry of Good News Publishers. Used by permission. All rights reserved.

FIRST EDITION

Dedication

This book is for all of those I have talked to over the years who found themselves standing at the threshold of change yet struggling with the thought of whether or not they were prepared to quit and say, "I'm ready!"

It is also for those who took the next step with courage, declaring, "I'm in." Both groups, in their unique ways, were critical in shaping my understanding of what is necessary and critical for success in this journey

Your honesty and your willingness to seek freedom have inspired every word of this book. May it serve as a guide and a beacon of hope for others as they discover the life God has prepared for them—one filled with His grace, strength, and promises of renewal.

With deep gratitude and faith, persevere.

Rose Ann Forte

Take the First Step Toward Your
Freedom!

Transformation begins with action.

To help you get the most out of each chapter and make the most of this journey, I've created a free companion workbook filled with practical exercises, reflective prompts, and tools to help you unlock the keys to a Spirit-filled life.

Scan the QR code below to access your *Prepare to Quit Workbook* and begin putting the pieces together—one key at a time.

This workbook is designed to:
- Guide you through the exercises in each chapter.
- Help you track your progress and reflections.
- Equip you with actionable steps for lasting change.

Don't wait—start unlocking your freedom today!

Prepare to Quit Workbook

By failing to prepare,
you're preparing to fail.

~ Benjamin Franklin ~

Contents

	Foreword by Karl Benzio	1
	Introduction	5
1	I Can't Keep Doing This	13
2	The Truth Will Set You Free	21
3	The Mirror Doesn't Lie	33
4	Mindset Matters	43
5	Visualize the Future	55
6	Choose an Accountability Method	65
7	Invest in Yourself	73
8	Make God a Part of Your Plan	83
9	Unlocking the Full Picture	93
	Notes	107
	About the Author	109

Foreword

Change is a journey—one that begins not in the moment of transformation but much earlier in the moment of preparation. The journey to freedom from alcohol or any destructive habit requires intentional steps, a clear vision, and a foundation built on truth—truth about ourselves, our Creator, and the purpose He designed for us.

Prepare to Quit is a lighthouse for those ready to embark on their healing journey. It aligns beautifully with the Transtheoretical Model of Change, which describes how individuals progress through five stages for transformation—from pre-contemplation (not wanting change) to contemplation (wanting change), then preparation (make a plan), action (plan in action), and finally maintenance (stable and continuing the plan). But this book does more than illuminate these steps—it connects them to the timeless wisdom of Scripture and the transformative power of a Spirit-filled life.

Rose Ann Forte, with her unique blend of personal testimony and biblical insight, has created a resource that practically addresses the whole person: spirit, mind, and body. She understands that quitting is not merely an act of the will but a process of renewal—one that requires us to rewire our neural pathways, embrace accountability, and anchor ourselves in God's promises.

What stands out most in this book is its focus on preparation—a stage often overlooked in recovery narratives but essential for lasting change. Rose Ann equips readers with practical tools and biblical truths to confront their habits, reflect on their choices, and visualize the future God has for them. In doing so, she helps them move from a place of psychological slavery to one of freedom, where their identity is no longer tied to dysfunctional choices but rooted in Christ.

Personally, if I had this book when I was ready to quit, it would have saved me so much hurt and lessened the pain of those I hurt. Professionally, as someone who has spent decades helping individuals overcome their addiction and mental health challenges, integrating faith and evidence-based science accelerates God's healing process. The steps outlined in this book not only simplify but also deeply empower, offering readers a sense of assured hope and agency as they prepare to say goodbye to alcohol.

To those holding this book: know that you are not alone in your struggle. If you're like me during my addiction, you're probably excited about moving forward. But to be honest, also nervous and fearful of some pain. That's okay. Even though both paths, forward or backward, can be painful, the God who created you sees your pain, your fears, and your desires for a better life. He has plans to prosper you and not to harm you, plans to give you hope and a future (Jeremiah 29:11).

Rose Ann's book delivers what ultimately propelled me to transformation, the peace of my life verse: He gives him perfect peace whose mind is fixed on Thee, because he trusts You (Isaiah 26:3). Rose Ann helps you keep your mind fixed on God, especially when the going gets tough.

This book embodies these two promises, guiding you step-by-step toward the life He has in store for you. May you find strength in these pages, courage in the journey ahead, and joy in the freedom that awaits.

by His grace,

Karl Benzio, MD
Medical Director
American Association of Christian Counselors

Rose Ann Forte

Introduction

Finding the Keys to Unlock a Spirit-Filled Life

Have you ever found yourself saying, *I can't keep doing this?* Maybe you've whispered it into the silence of the night or felt it rise in your heart after yet another day of struggle. Those words may feel like defeat, but they're actually the beginning of something powerful. They're a call to action, a recognition that life as it is right now is *not* what God intended for you. And most importantly those words are a step toward freedom.

But freedom isn't found in one big leap. It's unlocked, piece by piece.

This book is about finding the keys to your freedom—not just freedom from alcohol but freedom to live the life God designed for you—a life that is filled with peace, joy, purpose, and the unshakable knowledge that you are loved by your Heavenly Father.

As we journey through these pages together, you'll discover that this process is like piecing together a puzzle. The shape of that puzzle is no accident—it's a cross. The cross reminds us of Jesus' ultimate sacrifice and His promise of redemption. Each chapter of this book represents a key that unlocks a piece of that puzzle, drawing you closer to the complete picture of a Spirit-filled life, one that is free from the psychological slavery of this habit. Galatians 5:1 (NIV) tells us, "*It is for freedom that Christ has set us free. Stand firm, then, and do not let yourselves be burdened again by a yoke of slavery.*" Christ died on a cross for us to be *free*.

At the end of this journey, you'll hold all eight keys, and you'll have unlocked the final piece: *I'm ready*—ready to step forward, equipped with a God-centered faith, a practical guide, and a renewed mindset, into the life God has planned for you.

The Struggle Is Real, but So Is the Solution

For many of us, alcohol isn't just a drink—it has become a way to cope, a way to numb pain, or even a way to celebrate life's highs and lows. Over time, it takes more than it gives, leaving us feeling stuck, powerless, or ashamed.

If that's where you find yourself today, I want you to know two things:

1. You are not alone.

2. There is hope.

This book isn't about judgment or blame. It's about preparation. Quitting alcohol isn't something you rush into; it's something you prepare for. Just like a carpenter gathers tools before building or a runner trains before a marathon, you need to equip yourself for this journey. That's what this book is designed to help you do—prepare, step by step, until you're ready to say goodbye to alcohol and hello to the Spirit-filled life God has for you.

The Power of Keys

Why keys? Keys are powerful symbols. They represent access, opportunity, and freedom. When you hold the right key, locked doors suddenly swing open. Obstacles dissolve. New pathways emerge.

Throughout this book, you'll discover eight keys, each one unlocking a specific area of your life that needs attention, healing, or transformation. These keys are practical, spiritual, rooted in biblical truths, and scientifically proven strategies to prepare you to quit.

Here's what you'll unlock:

- **Embrace Truth** – The foundation for change starts with the truth about alcohol, the truth about the enemy's lies, and the truth of God's Word.

- **Take Inventory** – A reflective look at how this substance has impacted your relationships, health, productivity, and relationship to your Heavenly Father.

- **Mindset** – Understanding how habits are formed and how to redirect your thoughts to align with truth, hope, and possibility.

- **Future Focus** – Visualize the life that is possible when your body is freed from the psychological slavery of this habit.

- **Accountability** – Build a support system to walk alongside you.

- **Invest** – Prioritize self-care by making sure to invest in your health, well-being, and future.

- **God** – Center your plan around Him, relying on His strength and building a strong armor to resist temptation from the enemy.

- **I'm Ready** – Put all the pieces together and step forward in faith with Him.

Each chapter introduces one key and invites you to reflect, take action, and move closer to unlocking the full picture.

Why a Cross?

The cross is central to this journey because it's central to our faith. Jesus' death and resurrection were the ultimate keys to our freedom—freedom from sin, shame, and separation from God. As you unlock each piece of this puzzle, you're not just building a symbol; you're stepping into the truth of what the cross represents: new life, redemption, and unshakable hope. The cross holds the key to our deepest relationships—our connection with God reaching upward (vertical), our love and service to others extending outward (horizontal), and at the intersection, where the two meet, the transformation of self.

When the final piece of the puzzle is in place, you'll look back and see not just the steps you've taken to prepare to quit, but you will be excited about the transformation God will work in you, as you trust in Him and the promise He has for you. Jeremiah 29:11 (NIV) *"For I know the plans I have for you," declares the lord, "plans to prosper you and not to harm you, plans to give you hope and a future."*

Preparation is a Stage of Change!

True transformation begins long before the moment of change—preparation is not just a step, it is the foundation of success. Scientific models, such as the Transtheoretical Model of Change, affirm that lasting change follows a sequence of necessary steps: pre-contemplation, contemplation, and then preparation. This stage is where you gather the knowledge, tools, and faith needed to step into action with confidence.

You are not just hoping for change—you are actively building the path to it.

What to Expect

This journey is intended to walk you through a process with honest reflection and tools to empower you to say, "Enough is enough," so that you will not only be ready to quit, but you will also have the tools to be successful in doing so.

Remember, God's grace is sufficient for every moment. He provides new mercies and forgiveness every day of your life. Your path is secure in His promise that our salvation is protected when we put our faith in Him. His strength is made perfect in your weakness. 1 John 4:4 states: *"He who is within you is stronger than he who is in the world."*

Each chapter includes:

- **A Key** – A principle or action step that unlocks part of the puzzle.

- **Biblical Reflections** – Scripture to guide and inspire you.

- **Practical Exercises** – Tips to help you apply what you're learning.

- **Encouragement** – Truths to keep you motivated.

By the end of this book, you'll not only be prepared to quit alcohol, but you'll also be ready to embrace a life filled with purpose, joy, and the Holy Spirit.

Let's Begin

You don't have to have it all figured out. All you need is a willing heart and the courage to take the first step. God has already given you the keys to unlock the Spirit-filled life He has for you. Together, let's find them, use them, and discover the freedom that awaits.

Rose Ann Forte

1
I Can't Keep Doing This

The struggle you're in today is developing the strength you need for tomorrow. Don't give up.

~ Robert Tew ~

You Are Not Alone

Whether this is your first attempt to find freedom or you have tried and failed many times, know that *you are not alone.* Many people want to change their relationship with alcohol but find themselves breaking their own promises despite their best efforts. These troubling patterns not only apply to you, but they also apply to 10.9% of the US.[1] This means that for approximately every eleven people, one of them is struggling with how to moderate this substance. I would guess this statistic might be understated because this only represents those *reporting* a problem. As it turns out, many don't. Regardless of whether people report their drinking problem or not, what we now know is this: "…alcohol is now the leading driver of substance use-related fatalities nationwide."[2]

So, if you have picked up this book because you are finding it difficult to stop or manage your drinking, please know that you are in the company of a multitude of others trying to fight the same battle. Congratulate yourself for taking action to find the keys to unlocking a mindset that helps you *prepare to quit*. This walk is about empowering you to take control of your situation through a journey of processing truth and discerning the lies of society, the alcohol companies, and an enemy who roams this earth seeking to steal, kill, and destroy (1 Peter 5:8).

The reason you are here is clear. You have noticed consequences—severe ones—stemming from this false promise in a bottle. You've tried to manage it, negotiate with it, and put boundaries around it but haven't been able to achieve the self-control that you so desperately desire. That's when it hits you: "I can't keep doing this!"

I've had hundreds of conversations with people just like you who were struggling with this toxic substance and were worried. Fears, doubts, despair, and self-judgment are common. I've also spoken to countless Christians who keenly felt the burden of shame and guilt in their lives. They wondered why prayer and a Godly desire to change couldn't fix the problem. I've been in your shoes and felt the same shame, fears, and doubts. I struggled with this toxic substance for over a decade and wondered why I couldn't just stop. I was confused, embarrassed, and discouraged. This journey has helped me find what I believe are the most important keys to unlocking the critical pieces to *prepare to quit*.

My Story: Freedom From Psychological Slavery

I drank for decades, starting at the age of thirteen. Parties, socializing, work events, weddings, funerals, making dinner, kids' birthday parties, and so on. Drinking became my go-to for every imaginable situation. Alcohol was paired with every mood: happy or sad, stressed or relaxed. This was my number one way of coping in life. Yet, over time, it took *over* my life. My health suffered, my confidence dwindled, my relationships felt more disconnected, and I felt stuck.

Eventually, I realized I needed to make a change. I tried setting rules for myself, like only drinking on weekends, or the famous "just *one* tonight," but I kept breaking those promises. I felt ashamed and didn't want to ask for help because I didn't want to be labeled as an "alcoholic." While this is a completely acceptable term for many, for me, this word felt stigmatizing and prevented me from getting the help I needed (for maybe up to a decade).

It took a big wake-up call for me to finally decide to find freedom from the insidious grip alcohol had on my life. That wake-up call was the fear of getting fatally sick during the COVID-19 pandemic. I knew I had to take control of my health, and wine and spirits were getting in the way. I joined a 90-day coaching program that taught me new skills and provided the accountability I needed to stay alcohol-free, and my life started to change for the better.

What was most profound was the way God took my struggle and transformed it into something extraordinary. Romans 8:28 (NLT) tells us: *"And we know that God causes everything to work together for the good of those who love God and are called according to his purpose for them."* When I finally removed this destructive crutch from my life, I lost weight, my health improved, and I felt the power of the Holy Spirit within. I finally experienced true freedom and wanted to help others feel the same.

I felt called by the Holy Spirit to document my journey. I ended up writing *The Plans He Has For Me Daily Devotional* and authored two more books. All of this began at age 60 (after decades of excessive alcohol use). This experience captures the very important message *for everyone* that it is *never too late* for God's purpose to unfold. God has an incredible plan for each one of us and can use your story too. No one is excluded from this promise as we choose to obediently follow Him.

A Plan for Success

Unfortunately, a very small percentage of people who struggle with drinking receive help—less than 8%.[3] Most end up suffering in silence due to the stigma of admitting they have a problem. Yet, according to the World Health Organization, this most popular substance is a problem that affects a whopping 400 million people worldwide.[4] Again, I believe there is a strong possibility that even this number might be understated due to the lack of people's honesty about the subject.

I know from experience that there is a lot of fear that exists which prevents many people from taking that first step into freedom. This book was created to help you face those fears, shift your mindset, and find the keys to unlock your potential when you choose to quit. Whether you are taking a break for a spell (Dry January, Lent, Sober October, and so on) or you are going for a fully committed alcohol-free life, these pages are meant to set you up for success.

However, the foundation of any successful plan is self-awareness, which provides the clarity needed to understand where you are now and empowers you to begin the journey toward your alcohol-free goal. The keys that unlock the strategies that follow are a combination of carefully selected biblical scriptures, brain science, and evidence-based practices that best prepare you to quit successfully.

These concepts worked for me and countless others, and they can help you, too. Most importantly, each one included in these pages seeks to connect us to our ultimate source of strength: God.

Rose Ann Forte

2
The Truth Will Set You Free

All truths are easy to understand once they are discovered; the point is to discover them.

~ Galileo Galilei ~

The Truth About Alcohol

For a long time, the idea of questioning my relationship with alcohol seemed unnecessary. After all, it was always "those other people" who had problems. Drinking is not only socially acceptable but *not drinking* is often frowned upon. Although alcohol may provide pleasure, relieve stress, and seem integral to social, business, and family gatherings, it is actually a toxic substance that can wreak havoc on our health and our personal lives. Alcohol is also addictive, and that's when some troubling patterns start to emerge, and almost always, unexpectedly.

Embracing truth unlocks self-awareness, helping you see the hidden ways alcohol impacts your life. To find the truth, consider asking yourself the following questions:

- Does my alcohol use negatively affect my body, mind, and spirit?

- Does my drinking prevent me from becoming the best version of myself--the person I was created to be?
- Is my continual preoccupation with this substance interfering with my long-term goals?
- Has this thing become my idol (the thing I worship more than God)?
- Does alcohol take precedence over important relationships and other responsibilities?
- Am I less productive than I should be after a night of drinking?

Alcohol's Impact on The Body and Mind

Alcohol's impact on physical health is significant. Over time, it can harm your liver, heart, and other organs. The liver, a critical organ for filtering toxins, struggles under the burden of regular drinking, and long-term consumption can lead to liver damage. In fact, cirrhosis of the liver is expected to triple by the year 2030.[5] *Similarly*, your heart is affected. Regular and compulsive drinking can elevate blood pressure and contribute to heart problems, including heart attacks and strokes.[6]

Beyond the physical, the constant use of this sometimes-lethal substance also takes a toll on mental health. While it may provide a temporary escape or confidence boost, it often results in emotional crashes which contribute to anxiety, depression, and even more severe mental health issues. In addition, according to the Mental Health Foundation, excessive alcohol use can also increase cases of psychosis, suicide, and self-harm.[7]

Spiritual Consequences

When you are a person of faith, you certainly understand that pursuing this substance on a continual basis can make you feel completely disconnected from God and His plan for you. Repeated failed attempts, embarrassing behaviors, broken relationships, and lost productivity can all cause unwanted guilt and shame. The result is that you feel disconnected from your loving, Heavenly Father, not because He has turned away from you, but because your focus continually shifts away from Him. When you are under the influence, your focus is not on God, and the consequences can be, and usually are, severe. Embracing truth is the key to understanding the spiritual impact of alcohol and finding hope in restoration.

Shame Prevents Healing

While shame is a distinctive characteristic and result of the consequences of excessive alcohol use, it is also the enemy of healing from the psychological slavery that is being experienced. Shame comes from a worldly guilt that says, "there is something wrong with me and I'm not fixable." But Godly guilt is not about there being anything wrong or defective with you. It is about acknowledging that we've done something wrong and simply requires a repentant heart. It is the Holy Spirit's prompting of our need for forgiveness, which God freely grants. Believing that you are somehow defective is a strategy that comes from the enemy and this world.

Jesus went to the cross so our sins could be forgiven, and we could be restored to a place of being right with God. When shame is present, it means that you are disagreeing with God and discounting the gift you received from the sacrifice made on the cross. This line of thinking is worldly and comes from the enemy, not God. With respect to shame, let's obliterate it and choose to agree with God. Accept the forgiveness that is offered (each and every day) and look forward to a different future by lifting any burden related to your past.

By embracing truth, we gain access to the key that unlocks self-awareness so we can develop an understanding of any shame we may be carrying. This enables us to also unlock the hope that God's forgiveness offers, enabling true healing.

Understanding the Addictive Nature of Alcohol

Despite culture's acceptance, alcohol is highly addictive because it causes a higher-than-normal dopamine spike in neural transmitters. A neural transmitter is a chemical messenger in your brain and body. It helps pass signals between nerve cells so they can communicate and control things like your mood, thoughts, and movements. Dopamine is the "feel good" neurotransmitter designed by our creator so we can experience joy from activities we engage in. Alcohol's excessive dopamine release reinforces the desire to drink, creating a cycle that can lead to addiction. This makes it challenging for many to quit drinking without some sort of assistance. The National Institute on Alcohol Abuse and Alcoholism (NIAAA) is dedicated to research on the prevention and treatment of alcohol use disorder (addiction), and much of its research includes the effect on brain chemistry in areas responsible for memory, decision-making, impulse control, and attention.[8]

The Role of the Subconscious Mind

Understanding why it is so hard to quit alcohol involves recognizing the role of the subconscious mind in habit formation (creation of new neural pathways). Most of our actions are governed by the subconscious mind, which directs behaviors through habits and internal programming. Our subconscious mind is sensitive to triggers that it believes will give us rewards. According to Bruce Lipton, author of Biology of Belief, the subconscious mind operates about 90% of the time and is responsible for habitual behaviors that play automatically, without conscious thought.[9]

This automatic functioning is why all habits, including the reasons we choose to drink, become so ingrained. Our God-designed brains were created to save time and energy, producing new neural pathways that operate automatically from repetitive behaviors. This can be beneficial for habits like brushing your teeth or driving to and from work, but detrimental when applied to harmful behaviors like excessive drinking.

Finding Freedom from Psychological Slavery

The Bible warns us about the dangers of being a slave to sin. Jesus said in John 8:34 (ESV), *"Truly, truly, I say to you, everyone who practices sin is a slave to sin."* Alcohol dependency certainly feels like a form of slavery—psychological slavery! Despite wanting to quit, many feel like it is impossible because they have become imprisoned by their habit as a result of neural patterns that were formed from repeated use.

However, there is hope!

Science confirms that new neurological patterns can be created with mindset shifts in our awareness of new reward systems. In other words, our brains can make new pathways when we change how we think and focus on new ways to feel good about things. This is consistent with God's Word, as well. Romans 12:2 (NLT) states, *"Don't copy the behavior and customs of this world, but let God transform you into a new person by changing the way you think. Then you will learn to know God's will for you, which is good and pleasing and perfect."*

We can apply this wisdom to gain freedom from alcohol by understanding how our brains work. Creating new ways of thinking and decision-making around this substance can change the brain's physical structure. The brain's desire for a positive experience can be redirected to healthier activities and behaviors that better solve whatever solution we are looking for through alcohol (dealing with stress, anxiety, lack of connection, fearlessness, and so on). Repeated new behaviors create new neural pathways and God promises us that by testing things, we can renew our minds (Romans 12:2).

The Benefits of Living Alcohol-Free

While reducing the harm this substance causes is essential, the real motivation for quitting lies in the benefits of an alcohol-free life. Freedom from this psychological slavery leads to mental clarity, improved relationships, reduced inflammation, and personal growth. Most importantly, it will deepen your connection with God, giving you a new North Star to walk toward that allows you to discover the plans He has for you (Jeremiah 29:11).

Truth Is a Key to Freedom

The following chapters are designed to help you find the keys to unlocking the strategies to *prepare to quit* by understanding the science behind habit formation. They will use the truth of God's Word and the truth about how alcohol is affecting your body, mind, and soul. It will also identify your personal reasons for making a change and will aim to set the stage for success by equipping you with keys to the right tools to combat your seemingly incontrollable behavior surrounding this substance. So, find the key that unlocks that first step in truth toward freedom, and prepare yourself for a life that's not just lived but truly celebrated.

Rose Ann Forte

3
The Mirror Doesn't Lie

You can't go back and change the beginning, but you can start where you are and change the ending.

~ C.S. Lewis ~

Reflect on Your Past

The mirror not only reflects the present but also the past that shaped it. Choosing freedom begins with finding the key that unlocks reflection on the consequences of your past choices as they relate to alcohol, an essential part of the preparation process for quitting. This step is vital to successfully moving on from a substance that is hijacking your life because it establishes a clear understanding of the negative impacts, reinforces the reasons for change, and guides the formation of a committed and effective plan for quitting. This reflection on the past is *not* about indulging in regret. It's about harnessing insights that fuel your motivation for a better future. Taking inventory helps you see the full picture of alcohol's impact on your life.

Awareness is the first step in this process. Take inventory—grab a piece of paper and a pen. Think of the different categories of your life and assess the negative effects of alcohol. Relationships with family, connection to God, financial security, mental health, career, physical health, etc. How has this substance impacted these areas in a damaging way? Again, this question is not to shame or guilt, but to see the honest picture of how this substance has diminished the quality of your life.

Reflection on the past can expose a crooked path, paved with the negative consequences of choosing alcohol. Conversely, obedience to God can make crooked paths straight. There are frequent references in the Bible confirming this. Luke 3:5-6 (NLT) states: *"The valleys will be filled, and the mountains and hills made level. The curves will be straightened, and the rough places made smooth. And then all people will see the salvation sent from God."* In Isaiah 42:16 (NLT), we also see how some dark and crooked paths can be straightened with God at the helm: *"I will lead blind Israel down a new path, guiding them along an unfamiliar way. I will brighten the darkness before them and smooth out the road ahead of them. Yes, I will indeed do these things; I will not forsake them."*

The crooked path also symbolizes how we have lost our way in a forest of fears and excuses. Thankfully, God's Word offers a GPS out of the jungle, and that straight path is guided by TRUTH. Proverbs 10:9 (NLT) shares: *"People with integrity walk safely, but those who follow crooked paths will be exposed."*

Taking inventory means an honest look in the symbolic mirror. When you examine what your reflection reveals, you can find closure with your past and chart a better path forward. Let's explore some ways overindulgence in alcohol has affected your life and landed you on the crooked path.

Body

Common reasons to quit relate to lack of sleep, weight gain, and other health concerns. Puffy faces, high blood pressure, exhaustion, and low productivity because of lack of energy--do any of these symptoms sound familiar? Poor exercise and eating choices often accompany excessive alcohol consumption, as there is little to no energy for proper self-care. Drinking problems also can lead to added wrinkles and damaged skin.[10] Chronic consumption increases your chance of cancer and heart disease or accidental death. This is why, according to the US Centers for

Disease Control and Prevention report, alcohol is a leading cause of preventable death.[11] Perhaps most striking, the Surgeon General of the United States recently came out with a new advisory on the link between alcohol and cancer risk. In short, even moderate drinking is directly linked to a higher risk for seven different kinds of cancer.[12] Taking inventory of your health helps you see the physical cost of alcohol consumption.

Mind

Anxiety and depression go hand-in-hand when this idol has taken over. Many believe alcohol relieves these symptoms, but it only provides temporary numbness. The problems remain when the substance wears off. The National Institute of Health connects drinking with depression and anxiety: *"As a typical depressant, alcohol affects the brain in many ways, and it is likely that high doses will cause feelings of sadness (i.e., depression) during intoxication that evolve into feelings of nervousness (i.e., anxiety) during the subsequent hangover and withdrawal."*[13] How has this substance created a shift in your anxiety or your overall psychological well-being?

Relationships

Proverbs 20:1 (NLT) reveals how *"wine produces mockers"* and *"alcohol leads to brawls."* Have you ever argued with a friend, spouse, or significant other while intoxicated? Have you ever sent a text while under the influence and regretted it the next day? It's likely that your relationships have suffered. Worse yet, you might be isolating yourself to hide your consumption. Close and authentic connections with others will suffer when your relationship with wine, beer, or other liquor becomes more important. How have your relationships been affected because of this substance?

Financial

Spending money on this liquid poison can be expensive. An average bottle of wine costs between $15-$30 before tax, and at a restaurant, one glass could be $10-20 before tip. Other forms of liquor are not too far off from that. Hangovers and recovery lower our productivity and inhibit full performance at work. Lack of motivation can prevent seeking a raise or a better job, affecting income potential. Taking inventory of your finances can reveal the true financial cost of alcohol on your life. What is the real financial cost of your habit?

Overall Unhappiness

Proverbs 23:29-30 (NLT) connects anguish and sorrow with those who overindulge in substances that prevent sober-mindedness: *"Who has anguish? Who has sorrow? Who is always fighting? Who is always complaining? Who has unnecessary bruises? Who has bloodshot eyes? It is the one who spends long hours in the taverns, trying out new drinks."*

When alcohol has a grip on your life, regret permeates this habit, since most of us know and understand that we were created for something greater. We tend to dream big while under the influence, only to spend the next day nursing a hangover instead of taking steps toward our dreams. This gap between where we want to be and where we are can be unsettling.

Ultimately, this liquid assassin steals from many aspects of our lives: our physical and mental health, our relationships, our career performance, wealth potential, and much more. More importantly, our self-respect and spiritual confidence can erode as we struggle to control a substance, making God feel distant. This is not because God is absent, but because we have turned our back on Him. This is where you should applaud yourself for taking action to understand how to *prepare to quit*. Through this reflection process, you can see the many ways alcohol affects you and also get excited about how to vastly improve every aspect of your life!

Knowledge Is Power

Reflecting on the past is not about dwelling on it but learning from it. It's about understanding the role your drinking has played in your life and using that knowledge to empower your journey toward healing and a healthier future. It's a vital step in breaking the cycle, building resilience, and fostering sustainable change. Taking stock of the consequences of your drinking is a key strategy that unlocks your motivation to change.

Reflecting on your past in a mature and honest way will allow you to see how a substance has affected various aspects of your life. It can create a sense of urgency and a clear reason for change. It can provide excitement for a different future and uncover a better plan, one that God can help reveal.

By identifying the negative consequences of alcohol, you are reminded of what you stand to lose if you continue indulging and what you will gain by quitting. This understanding can serve as a powerful motivator. Continued reflection, without shame or guilt, reinforces the value of the journey toward freedom from the psychological slavery of this habit. This reflection is a continuous process, serving as a guide and reminder throughout the journey of healing, helping you remain committed, learning from the past, and building a healthier future.

Rose Ann Forte

4
Mindset Matters

If you do what you've always done, you'll get what you've always gotten.

~ Tony Robbins ~

The Lies We Tell Ourselves

"Our life is always moving in the direction of our strongest thoughts," according to Craig Groschel, a prominent American pastor, author, and speaker. Scripture supports the connection between thoughts and behavior, encouraging us to take our thoughts captive (2 Corinthians 10:5). Being aware of your thoughts gives access to the key that unlocks a growth mindset. This turns challenges into opportunities. Perspective and belief systems dictate behaviors and outcomes. That is why reframing how you think and preparing ahead for potential obstacles is essential when *preparing to quit.*

Has liquor become your golden calf? Has your drinking habit consumed most of your focus--coming before God, your dreams, your family, and your physical and psychological wellbeing? For many, the invisible line was crossed long before we realized it. And this can feel frightening. Nobody wants to feel like they've lost control.

Most of us don't wake up and say, "Hey, I really want to be a heavy drinker one day." No, that path starts off innocently enough, then lures us along in cunning methods that cause a lot of self-deception along the way. That is why the words of John 8:32 (NLT) are so powerful: *"And you will know the truth, and the truth will set you free."*

True freedom is found by finding the key that unlocks shedding light on the dark places and on the lies from the enemy to create a new mindset. That means facing the reality of our present with a willingness to change our course and do the right thing. The truth really can set you free. As you begin this journey, ask yourself:

- *Is there anything about your life right now that you have been unwilling to see honestly?*
- *Are there substances or behaviors stealing your focus away from God?*

Where Past Meets Present

In the last chapter, we discussed reflecting on your past. Reflecting on your past is crucial for self-awareness, learning, and motivating change as you move on from this substance that is wreaking havoc on your life. Equally important is reflecting on your present, which focuses on your current thoughts, behaviors, and circumstances to provide an immediate understanding of your relationship with alcohol today.

This involves catching the lies we tell ourselves (thoughts) so we can justify our drinking. When we know this toxin is harming our body, mind, spirit, and life potential, but we continue to make excuses so we can keep it around, we can fall into a pattern of what is called "cognitive dissonance." Cognitive dissonance is a term used in psychology for the phenomenon of believing two competing (and almost simultaneous) thoughts about the same thing. In its simplest form, cognitive dissonance happens with a substance when you understand the negative effects of it *(I hate it! I need to quit! It's so bad for me!)* while also holding the belief that it provides everything you need in life, and you can't live without it. Take a moment to reflect on your relationship with alcohol and the lies you may have told yourself to understand how accurate they are. Common examples are *I need a drink to relax; wine reduces my anxiety; a few beers help me socialize;* or, *I'll just have one.* Your mindset matters when you are able to redirect your thoughts towards truth.

When you look at these statements and compare them to reality, you will find some massive contradictions. For example, alcohol is known to *cause* stress and anxiety in the long term, can isolate people instead of connecting them authentically to others, and most find it impossible to stop at just one drink. Keep tabs on your excuses, fears, and outright lies that want to bring you back to drinking. Remember, no one says, "I'm so glad I gave in last night--it feels great to be at day one again!" Getting a handle on and solving for cognitive dissonance will unlock the puzzle piece related to finding a growth mindset.

Habits Feel Hard to Break... at First

Part of why you might get stuck when it comes to getting rid of this hijacking influence in your life is that change feels uncomfortable. It's a brain thing--it's because of our mind's process of habit formation. Our brain loves to save energy, so it goes into autopilot whenever it can. We get hardwired, so when habits are formed, repeated behaviors are fast and easy (cue brushing your teeth or even driving to work -- you don't think too much about how to do these, you just do them automatically).

Repetitive behaviors create neural pathways that are like well-worn paths through a forest. It's much easier to take the trail than bushwhack to find a new one. These "paths" make it easier for the brain to perform these behaviors automatically, without much thought or effort. So, understand that breaking your drinking habit will feel uncomfortable *at first*, but it gets easier as time progresses. When someone tries to change a deeply ingrained relationship with a substance, they are not only up against their body's physical reliance on it (luckily, this discomfort goes away within two weeks to a month), they are also going up against a neurological pathway that has been built around it.

Creating a New Normal

Just as paths in a forest become overgrown if they're not used, neural pathways can also weaken over time when they're not engaged. By consistently practicing new, healthier behaviors and avoiding the former habitual activity, you're allowing those old pathways to diminish while building new ones. This process is often referred to as "neuroplasticity," which is the brain's ability to form and reorganize synaptic connections, especially in response to a new learning or experience.

The key to unlocking this new mindset is rooted in practice. This key unlocks a mindset of growth and freedom, as consistent practice reshapes your neural pathways and strengthens your new, alcohol-free identity. Changing a habit gets easier each day you practice your new routine (not drinking!) because creating a new habit is about repetition and persistence. Each time you choose the new behavior over the old, you're strengthening the new neural pathway and creating a new mindset, making it easier and more natural for your brain to follow this path in the future. Over time, the new behavior becomes more automatic, and the urge to engage in the old behavior diminishes. The important message here is the more time you put into creating your new narrative that creates new substance-free choices, the more your brain responds and changes. That means you will experience triggers less over time.

Identify Your Triggers and Cravings

Expect triggers and cravings. The more awareness you put into your potential challenges—and plan accordingly—the more you can develop a new mindset that makes your substance-free efforts count. You know yourself better than anyone. You also probably know the tricks or triggers that could get in the way of your goal to find freedom from alcohol. This awareness can help you assess your present in a much more effective way. For example, are there certain people you may want to avoid in the first few weeks of abstinence because you associate them with alcohol? Should you avoid certain physical locations because they trigger your desire to drink? Do you need to take a different road home to avoid the places where you buy your favorite poison? Thinking this through is a game changer for your future success when choosing to free yourself from the psychological slavery of this habit. This key unlocks a mindset that says: "I'm prepared and committed."

Choose Your Hard

Ultimately, it can feel hard to quit at first, *but it is also hard to keep drinking.* Imagine if you *never* stop consuming this substance. What does that future look like?

One path may be hard over the short-term while the other path will be hard over a lifetime. Therefore, use wisdom and truth when developing your new mindset and "choose your hard." A growth mindset means embracing the short-term difficulty of quitting for the long-term reward of a healthier, alcohol-free life.

Lasting freedom from the psychological slavery of alcohol is worth taking a step into the temporary discomfort of quitting drinking. With each progressive day you choose freedom, your brain's new neural pathways get stronger. Scripture encourages you to be persistent and not give up, because blessings await you. Galatians 6:9 (NLT) states, *"So, let's not get tired of doing what is good. At just the right time we will reap a harvest of blessing if we don't give up."* Unexpected gifts are on the other side of this journey! It is worth it, and it gets easier with each day and each moment you choose freedom.

Harnessing the Power of the Present

In conclusion, reflecting on the present is the key that provides a powerful tool in developing a mindset that *prepares you to quit*. It involves awareness of one's current state, recognizing the lies we have told ourselves, and identifying potential triggers. It puts the consequences of using the substance in proper perspective. This focus on "now" is instrumental in being able to make informed decisions, develop effective coping strategies, and maintain motivation and commitment to a substance-free life. By staying grounded in the present, individuals can use this key to unlock the mindset of preparedness for the journey of freedom ahead.

Rose Ann Forte

5
Visualize The Future

If you don't think about the future, you cannot have one.

~ John Galsworthy ~

FUTURE FOCUS

The Fork in the Road

Are you at a crossroads? Look at your life. Can you see one path that holds the promise of a brighter future, while the other is already filled with broken promises and regrets? The challenge is, that even if you're unhappy with the path you're on, taking that first step away from alcohol can feel scary. But know this: You are not alone—it's natural to feel drawn to the familiar, even when a better way is possible. This is why future focus is essential. Keeping your eyes on the brighter path ahead gives you the courage to take the first step away from the familiar and into God's promises.

If you are stuck at this crossroads, consider this book a direct line of encouragement for you to take that step toward freedom. You won't be disappointed! Jeremiah 29:11 (NIV) promises, *"For I know the plans I have for you... plans for good and not for disaster, to give you a future and a hope."* God does envision a better future for you when you follow

Him—a life that reflects the best version of you that is not held back by a bottle.

Focus On a Future Filled with Promise

There is a big difference between getting away from something negative versus moving towards something attractive. That's why finding the key to unlocking a future-focused mindset rooted in God's promise is essential. This future-focused mindset concentrates on the better life God has designed for you. This is about living a life of peace and joy, despite circumstances and, more importantly, a life free from the psychological slavery produced by alcohol. Future focus shifts your mindset from what you're leaving behind to the incredible blessings and opportunities awaiting you when you step into God's plan for your life.

When we idolize beer, wine, or any other liquor over God, we miss out on developing our God-given gifts and talents, building deep relationships, and experiencing and showing the love of the Holy Spirit to others. When we can flip the narrative on how a substance is holding us back and dream of what's possible without it, we can develop the incentive to persevere in times of trials and temptations. It's the exact motivation we need to make it to the other side.

Recognizing Your God-Given Gifts

This journey is about so much more than giving up a bad habit. God has given each of us unique gifts and talents. YOU are an incredible creation! In Luke 12:7 (NLT), Jesus shares that God knows you intimately: *"And the very hairs on your head are all numbered. So don't be afraid; you are more valuable to God than a whole flock of sparrows."* Dousing that potential in alcohol prevents you from finding and activating those gifts from God, who considers you precious, special, and unique.

Quitting this substance is not just about removing a negative influence--it's about unleashing all the positive things you're capable of doing. In other words, when you are free from the grips of alcohol, you get to use these God-given gifts to their full potential. Concentrating on the future when quitting drinking is like setting a GPS for a healthier, happier and more peaceful destination. You are no longer just avoiding your idol; you are moving toward a future that was designed for you by God, where your gifts are used for His purpose.

Visualize Your Why

Reflecting on your past and present helps you clarify why quitting is so important. But it's your future focus that gives you the motivation to keep going, envisioning what God has in store for you beyond this moment. Visualizing your future ignites excitement about what's possible when you embrace the independence of an alcohol-free life. Just as you focused on the costs of intoxication, now you can dream about the rewards that will come when you choose freedom.

When you start focusing on your future, you can push forward with greater momentum with the big picture in mind. Romans 12:12 reminds us to "*rejoice in hope*," and to cultivate enthusiasm about the plans He has for you. This hope and enthusiasm become our fuel to drive us forward, and it also becomes our strength when we face challenges. These plans often include what we have longed for in our hearts, but these plans also include joyful surprises we could never have anticipated (the Creator of the universe has awesome ideas!).

Rely on God's Promises for Something Better through Scripture

Staying in scripture unlocks the key that keeps your future focus strong and reminds you that you are not doing this solo—the Holy Spirit is guiding you. And God has promised us something better when we cling to Him. Here are some reassuring passages to reflect on:

- Philippians 4:13 (NLT) confirms that you are not alone and have the power of the Holy Spirit: *"For I can do everything through Christ, who gives me strength."*
- 1 Peter 1:6-7 (NLT) encourages us to persevere: *"So be truly glad. There is wonderful joy ahead, even though you must endure many trials for a little while. These trials will show that your faith is genuine…"*

- Psalms 16:11 (NLT) reminds us that God will show us the way of life, granting us joy in the process: *"You will show me the way of life, granting me the joy of your presence and the pleasures of living with you forever."*

These passages of scripture can provide comfort and motivation. Staying in God's Word keeps you connected with your source of strength, the Holy Spirit, and will remind you daily that He is guiding you. God's Word plays a crucial role in keeping your future-focused mindset strong. If you are seeking further daily scripture and support, daily readings from *The Plans He Has For Me Daily Devotional* can provide the daily scriptural motivation to propel you forward, keeping God's promises at the forefront of your journey. This process helps you gain momentum, allowing hope to fuel your progress.

A Fresh Start with God's Grace

Visualizing the future isn't just about resetting your course—it's about leaving the past behind and embracing the fresh start God offers. Doesn't a fresh start sound wonderful? When you decide to take that alternative path, you get to leave that old life behind. The gift of forgiveness provided by the sacrifice on the cross is what gives you access to this fresh start.

Hebrews 10:17 (NLT) provides the assurance that God, after repentance, no longer remembers our past mistakes: *"I will never again remember their sins and lawless deeds."* In Philippians 3:13 (NLT), the Apostle Paul also tells us to leave our past behind: *"...forgetting the past and looking forward to what lies ahead, I press on to reach the end of the race and receive the heavenly prize for which God, through Christ Jesus, is calling us."* In this verse, Paul gives us the most authentic look at what it means to leave the past in the past, as he was a mass murderer of Christians himself before his conversion as a Christ follower.

When you choose freedom from alcohol, you're not only quitting drinking—you're creating a new chapter in your life and a new story to be used in your testimony. By focusing on the future, you step away from past regrets through forgiveness and start something new. You have found the key to creating a life full of possibilities, purpose, and a renewed sense of self-worth, rooted in God's grace.

Rose Ann Forte

6
Choose an Accountability Method

Accountability is the glue that ties commitment to the result.

~ Bob Proctor ~

Embracing Community and Commitment

Accountability to a wider community embraces the idea that *"What's mentionable is manageable."* Keeping our fears, struggles, and worries in the dark exacerbates the problem. When we keep our struggles hidden, fear and shame can take root, keeping us trapped. But when we share our burdens, we can open a path to healing. The Bible reinforces the power of supporting each other in Galatians 6:2 (NLT): *"Share each other's burdens, and in this way obey the law of Christ."* Allowing light into dark places is an essential step toward freedom.

Use this key to unlock an accountability strategy because it is a fundamental ingredient to genuine transformation. Accountability allows you to bring something that has been in the darkness (hiding your problem) into the light (sharing your journey with your support network). In this way, accountability is not just about sharing; it's about inviting others to stand with you, helping you stay on the path to freedom. Matthew 18:20 (NLT) reminds us God is present in community: *"For where two or three gather together as my followers, I am there among them."*

Strategies for Building Accountability

Share your decision to be alcohol-free (even if it's a commitment to do so for a short time) with trusted friends and family. Having people in your corner provides support when challenges arise. For example, if you're attending an event, let a few close people know so they can check in with you during an event or afterward. This added layer of accountability can be a game-changer when you're faced with tricky social situations.

Holding yourself accountable also means shifting your mindset from a deprivation point of view to a reward point of view. Having the right accountability tribe can keep you focused on mutual support and cheerleading, celebrating successes along the way. In other words, when you choose to live without alcohol and share that goal with others, you are more likely to focus on what you are *gaining* rather than what you are leaving behind. John 10:10 reminds us that Jesus came to give us a rich and satisfying life. This journey isn't about depriving ourselves. It's about embracing a healthier, more purposeful existence. Alcohol can often mask deeper issues and steal joy, but God's plan for us includes freedom, peace, and a purposeful future.

Using the Holy Spirit as Your Accountability Partner

God's Word serves as a reminder of God's plan and the joy that can follow when we trust in Him, using the Holy Spirit as our accountability partner. Here are a few verses to meditate on during this journey:

- Jeremiah 29:11 (NIV): *"For I know the plans I have for you, declares the Lord, plans for proper you and not harm you, plans to give you hope and a future."* God has our back and is planning for our success--not our downfall.
- Psalm 119:105 (NLT): *"Your word is a lamp to my feet and a light to my path."* His Word is our guide,

lighting up the path ahead, even when it seems a bit foggy.

- Psalm 37:4 (NLT): *"Take delight in the Lord and He will give you your heart's desire."* Trust in Him to provide what you need to fill your heart, soul and mind with peace and joy, despite circumstances.

Being accountable to God means embracing your choice to be free of alcohol, not because you feel obligated to abstain. It's not about the fact that you "should" abstain or "can't" drink. It's about recognizing that you *get to* choose a healthier, more fulfilling life.

Practical Accountability Options

There are a variety of practical ways to hold yourself accountable on a personal and community level when you're on the journey to becoming alcohol-free. The key is finding the right mix of support and commitment that works for you. Whichever method you choose, remember that consistent accountability is the foundation of lasting change. Here are some accountability ideas outside of friends and family to help you in your planning to quit:

- **Connect with other church members:** Whether it's a formalized program like Celebrate Recovery or Recovery Alive, a small group experience, bible study, or connecting via volunteerism, being with other like-minded Christians is a solid way to gain support and accountability. If not in a formalized *quit-drinking* support group, let people know you are putting down alcohol for a short period of time to focus on your body, mind, and spirit as a way to hold yourself accountable. It's not necessary to say "forever" at the beginning. It's just a way to share that you are doing something healthier for yourself.
- **Join online support groups:** Online forums offer support and encouragement. These can be found through Facebook, cell phone apps, web-based organizations, and countless other options. This option works well when you are *making every effort to fully engage and participate in them.*

- **Engage in alcohol-free programs:** Faith-based and non-faith-based programs that have a cost associated with them offer structured coaching and/or counseling tailored to an alcohol-free journey. These programs provide accountability through group sessions, one-on-one coaching or counseling, and online communities, ensuring you have the professional support you need to stay the course.

- **Journal daily:** Journaling is a conversation with yourself to track progress. You are encouraged to journal your feelings and progress prior to and during any alcohol cessation attempt. Journaling works as a complement to other accountability methods. Consider *The Plans He Has For Me Daily Devotional* for your journaling as it provides a simple structure with scriptural guidance, prayer, and prompts that are evidence-based in creating lasting change and new neural pathways as they relate to substance problems.

- **Join a local support group:** Alcoholics Anonymous, Celebrate Recovery and Recovery Alive are a few of the more well-known groups that provide a supportive in-person community. These programs provide a sponsor for accountability as well. In addition, there are many other local groups, like SMART Recovery and Salvation Army, that can be found through online research.

Keep Trying Until You Find the Perfect Match

Remember, there's no one-size-fits-all solution here. When you are planning to quit, keep in mind that it's about trying different things and seeing what resonates with you. Whether you choose to attend a meeting, jot down your thoughts, or connect with others in person or online, each step you take will provide you with a methodology of support that is critical to succeeding in any attempt to quit.

7
Invest In Yourself

If you really want to do something, you'll find a way. If you don't, you'll find an excuse.

~ Jim Rohn ~

The Pandemic's Drinking Crisis

If the pandemic taught us anything, it's the value of investing in ourselves and our well-being to face life's unexpected challenges. The pandemic was a scary time, especially if your relationship with alcohol took a darker turn. For many, this habit was pushed from a casual ritual or a manageable problem into something far more troublesome. As everything shut down around us, liquor stores stayed open and were deemed essential. In a short space of time, nightly cocktails became afternoon or even morning ones after lockdowns began.

Can you relate? If so, you wouldn't be alone. In a National Institutes of Health report, *Risky Alcohol Use: An Epidemic Inside the COVID-19 Pandemic*, nearly 25% of people reported heavy drinking during the pandemic, with alcohol-related deaths increasing by 38%. CNN highlighted the surge in overconsumption spurred by the pandemic in the article "The Pandemic May Have Created A Nation of Problem Drinkers – And Many Are Women."[14]

During the pandemic, I had to face a harsh truth: I had completely lost control of my drinking routines and behaviors, and I knew I didn't want to end up as another COVID-19 statistic. I needed a way out, and I found it through a coaching program. While the price I paid initially seemed steep as someone who was not working (retired), it became an invaluable investment in my life and a remarkable and wonderful form of self-care. Since finding freedom from my psychological slavery to alcohol, I have made that investment back 100-fold. I've transformed my health, career, self-esteem, and relationships. Most importantly, I have deepened my faith and connection to God.

But investing in oneself isn't always an easy transition. However, it is one of the important keys to unlocking freedom from this substance. For many, putting aside time or money for self-care feels unnecessary, wasteful, indulgent, or even selfish. However, just as you must put on your oxygen mask before helping others, dedicating time and investing in your well-being allows you to show up better for everyone else. While it may not seem intuitive, taking care of yourself first through self-care practices gives others the extraordinary gift of more of "you."

Understanding Self-Care

Self-care can look different for each of us—committing to a fitness routine, paying for counseling or coaching sessions, going back to school, or learning a new skill. Self-care also involves seeking support in overcoming challenges, like quitting a vice. Neglecting self-care because it costs money (or time) can make healing harder and take longer. Quite frankly, and in my experience, a person's unwillingness to invest in themselves in this area is almost always more costly in all areas of life in the long run. In addition, if you have been spending money on drinking while saying you can't afford a self-care regimen, a program, or a process to help you quit, then you might need to take a more reflective stance on what you are able to afford right now.

The reality is that you have been affording it. This habit has already cost you plenty of money and plenty of unproductive time. And, whether or not it has yet shown up in a meaningful way at this point, the truth is that it has cost you your health and psychological well-being. So, investing in yourself is simply diverting financial resources away from something that is reducing the quality or length of your life to something that will help you create a healthier and more joyful version of yourself. If you are interested in calculating the anticipated years of life lost due to drinking, consider using this assessment: https://americanaddictioncenters.org/effects-of-addiction-calculator

What price do you want to put on your relationships, your psychological well-being, your productivity, or your health and longevity? Whatever answer you get, add it to the direct cost of the alcohol you've been purchasing to understand what you truly can afford in the area of self-care practices.

Where we spend our money is an indication of what we think is important. When we invest in ourselves, we are demonstrating to ourselves that we matter. This is an expression of self-care and self-love.

It is also a very powerful form of accountability because what we invest in is what we pay close attention to. So, whether it's a life coach or counselor, personal trainer, healthy cooking class, or a program to help you quit drinking, don't be afraid to use this key to unlock this gift of freedom.

The Life-Changing Benefits of Investing in Yourself

Investing in yourself can be one of the most rewarding choices you can make because it helps you achieve the goals that matter most to you. In a *Forbes* article, "Why You Should Invest in Yourself," author Amy Modglin emphasizes the transformative power of investing in yourself, especially when you are pursuing personal growth or a significant life goal like quitting alcohol. The article shares how overcoming self-doubt, surrounding yourself with positive influences, and taking advantage of available resources can be a game changer, despite initial fears or financial concerns. In other words, your progress can be more profound. By committing time, effort, and finances to personal development, individuals can unlock their potential and achieve long-term success.[15]

Clint Haynes describes investing in yourself as a powerful step toward personal growth, well-being, and success in his article, "The Top 5 Benefits to Investing in Yourself." The author shares how investing is an important way to grow and improve your life. It helps you feel more confident, learn new skills, and share what you know with others. Even if it feels scary or selfish at first, taking care of yourself can make your relationships better and give you strength and accountability to handle difficult times. This can lead to a happier and more successful life.[16]

Both of these articles capture the research-based theme that investing in yourself is a powerful tool for creating a better future. This process begins with overcoming doubts and prioritizing self-care. Although you may worry in the moment about the time and financial investment required, research shows this investment pays off.

A Change in Perspective

Investing in yourself may feel challenging, especially if it demands resources you'd rather allocate elsewhere. However, prioritizing an investment in self-care (whether holistic or substance focused) is essential if you're committed to finding true freedom from the psychological slavery of this substance.

The way we spend our time and money reflects our values. Often, seeing how much goes toward maintaining a drinking habit can be a wake-up call. Imagine how different your life could be if that time and money were invested in your well-being, health, and faith journey instead.

What are You Waiting For?

Really. What are you waiting for? Dr. Jordan B. Peterson asks the question, *"Can you imagine yourself in 10 years if, instead of avoiding the things you know you should do, you actually did them every single day?"*[17] What a powerful approach. Yet, often, we will agonize over spending money on a worthy cause that could transform our lives while dumping cash daily—

without thinking twice—on harmful substances and toxic habits. The road to healing requires support, focus, and sometimes, financial sacrifice. But know that every effort is an investment in a better future.

Rose Ann Forte

8

Make God Part of Your Plan

God has not called me to be successful;
He has called me to be faithful.

~ Mother Teresa ~

A Turning Point in the Journey

For many, the relationship with alcohol begins innocently experimenting with peers, celebrating holidays, unwinding after work, or simply as a way to escape. And this is easy, even for a faith-focused person, based on the fact it's so socially acceptable. Yet, there often comes a point where the line is crossed, and this so-called "friend" begins to show its true colors. As this substance shifts from comfort to poison, it doesn't just damage health but also drains happiness and pulls our focus away from God and life's deeper purpose.

This is where the Holy Spirit steps in, filling you with conviction to break free from this life hijacker. The struggle becomes real when you can't imagine life without alcohol and the thought of continuing without it feels unbearable, making you feel like you are locked in a prison cell. The good news? You don't have to fight this battle alone. Shifting your focus back to God can find you the best key to unlock the strength you need to reclaim your life. As a matter of fact, 84% of scientific studies show that faith has a positive impact on addiction prevention and recovery.[18] In other words, God is a powerful part of the healing process!

When the will of God becomes your guiding light, freedom over alcohol becomes clear. Aligning your journey with Him illuminates the lies and false promises that come with temptation, leaving no doubt about your path forward.

From Self-Motivation to Spiritual Conviction

Initially, the motivation to quit drinking often stems from personal reasons—improving health, being a better role model, or saving money. However, a deeper conviction emerges when you realize that *drinking opposes your relationship with God.* Aligning your journey to freedom with God's truth transforms the process into a spiritual awakening.

1 John 1:5-7 (NLT) reminds us, *"God is light, and there is no darkness in him at all. So we are lying if we say we have fellowship with God but go on living in spiritual darkness; we are not practicing the truth. But if we are living in the light, as God is in the light, then we have fellowship with each other, and the blood of Jesus, his Son, cleanses us from all sin."* Living in the light requires honesty, accountability, and reliance on God's grace. Aligning our actions with the light of God's truth must be at the foundation of this journey.

This scripture is both an "ouch" and a blessing to understand. It reminds us that when we are not sober-minded, we live in spiritual darkness. We are not practicing His truth, and we're not inspiring others for the Kingdom. Yet the importance of community and accountability are also revealed here, both vital in quitting drinking. In this verse, John talks about having fellowship with one another and living in the light. Conquering this "thing" is close to impossible if we merely sit back in the darkness of our own thoughts and beat ourselves up for our struggles.

The good news is that the truth of God's Word and the truth of your circumstances will set you free if you are willing to self-reflect with integrity. This means openly acknowledging the problem—bringing what's in the darkness to light. This is where the Holy Spirit and faith-based community can make a huge difference in helping you move forward. This verse also reminds us of the sacrifice Jesus made on the cross when it reminds us that the blood of Jesus cleanses us from all sins. Every single day of our lives, this gift helps us start anew.

Ways to Put God First in Your Journey

The following key strategies will unlock the practical steps of building and maintaining a strong relationship with your Heavenly Father. God is the unwavering and ultimate source of strength and guidance in overcoming struggles with alcohol.

Spend Time in His Word: God's Word is *living and breathing (Hebrews 4:12)*, offering new insights with every reading. Regularly meditating on Scripture creates space for connection, guidance, and Godly discernment.

Practice Daily Prayer: Prayer is the cornerstone of a personal relationship with God, and it cultivates our faith and reliance on God's strength to get you through challenging times. 1 Thessalonians 5:17 (NLT) encourages us to *"Never stop praying."* Saying the Lord's Prayer slowly and mindfully is a simple yet powerful way to anchor yourself in prayer each day. Create a daily routine that incorporates prayer because this commitment will help solidify your relationship with Him.

Follow Your North Star: What is guiding your actions—your will or God's will? You already understand that your North Star is not meant to land in the place of chronic overindulgence of alcohol, or that you were born to numb out in some way to avoid pain. Redirecting your life's compass toward God keeps you aligned with His purpose for you. Recalibrating your focus toward Him helps dismantle worldly distractions so that your choices will be more closely aligned with the love that is expressed to you through your Heavenly Father.

Stay Connected Through Service: Making time to use your God-given gifts for the Kingdom is a game-changer. Serving others using your gifts strengthens your connection to Him and ignites purpose. Try volunteering in your church, mentoring, or exploring volunteer opportunities through your personal interests and passions. Be assured that God has a plan for all of us. Finding ways to serve is a way to be Christ-like and share that unique and special gift that was given to each of us.

Cultivate Gratitude: Being grateful for what we have instead of always wanting more is biblical and brings us closer to God. Ezra 3:11 tells us that people sang to the Lord with thanks, and Psalms 7:17 and 9:1 talk about thanking God wholeheartedly. God is our ultimate provider, so focusing on our thankfulness to God for what we have is a beautiful reminder that good things are not random. A practice of thanksgiving and gratitude in our daily lives is the proverbial "glass half full" approach, as this process creates a narrative that looks for something good in all situations.

Find a Church You Love: Fellowship is essential. A supportive church community provides encouragement, accountability, and shared values. Galatians 6:2 (NLT) reminds us to *"Share each other's burdens, and in this way obey the law of Christ."* If you haven't found the right church, keep exploring until you do. Scripture encourages us to find a supportive community where members help each other keep God at the center of their focus.

It's worth mentioning here that *The Plans He Has For Me Daily Devotional* was designed to help readers develop a daily practice of connecting with God as they put alcohol aside for twelve weeks. This resource combines daily prayer, scripture, gratitude journaling, and a self-reflection exercise to keep you focused on freedom from alcohol and connected to the Holy Spirit.

Living in the Light

Breaking free from alcohol's grip isn't just about abstaining; it's about stepping into the light of God's truth and living a life that honors Him. Each moment spent in prayer, service, gratitude, and fellowship strengthens your resolve and deepens your relationship with God.

Remember, this journey isn't about perfection; it's about progress. As you take steps to put God first, you'll discover the incredible transformation He has in store for you. Trust in His plan, lean on His strength, and let Him guide you into the life He's promised.

Rose Ann Forte

9

Unlocking the Full Picture

One day, you'll tell your story of how you overcame what you went through, and it will be someone else's survival guide.

~ Brené Brown ~

Are You in the Whale?

Was there a point when you realized the joy and relaxation you once found in drinking had long evaporated, replaced by 3 a.m. wakeups, relentless hangovers, and consuming shame? Worse still, do you feel your relationship with God growing distant, obscured by the veil of alcohol that clouded your connection with the Holy Spirit?

One of the greatest traps in preparing to quit is thinking there is actually a *right time* to do it. For many reading this book, the right time to quit was many years ago. The next best time is today. Unfortunately, thoughts like, "Maybe this isn't the best time for this" or "I can do this in a few months, instead of now," easily slide in, uninvited.

If you are feeling like God is calling you to end your relationship with alcohol, it is time to stop running away. Jonah ran from God and ended up inside the belly of a whale for 3 days. This bible story in the book of Jonah reminds us that God pursues us relentlessly, until we finally say, "I'm ready!" Those *day one again* promises, on repeat, are brutal. Each time we slip, we find ourselves back inside the whale, running from God while clinging to the false comfort of alcohol.

Knowledge Takes Your Power Back

This roller coaster is not unique to you. This is a real issue that tens of millions of problem drinkers face (hundreds of millions worldwide), stemming not only from our disobedience with God's will, but also from not understanding how our God-designed brains work. The more you understand the biology of habit formation and substance dependency, the more control and power you can yield with the help of the Holy Spirit.

Change is not a comfortable process *initially*; otherwise, so many people just like you would already be free. That is why we encourage you to take an active part in educating yourself. The more you know, the better equipped you are at combating your brain's attempt to sabotage your efforts to give up alcohol.

Applying the principles of habit formation and change, with the help of the Holy Spirit and the full armor of God, can provide the empowering tools to overcome psychological slavery.

It is Never Too Late to Transform Your Life

One essential lesson to learn is that it is never too late to completely transform your life. Philippians 1:6 (NLT) *"And I am certain that God, who began a good work within you, will continue his work until it is finally finished on the day when Christ Jesus returns."* God will use you and your story for His purpose until the day you take your last breath, or when Jesus returns… whichever is sooner.

It does not matter how many times you have attempted to quit. It's merely all part of your story. Leave the past in the past (through the gift of forgiveness offered from the cross) and start trusting in a new story that will be your testimony for others. When you declare, "I'm ready," you open the door to God's healing work in your life, regardless of how many times you've started over.

Temptation is the Opposite of Wisdom

We all know the metaphor of a lightbulb flashing over someone's head to signify a great idea. Think of increasing that inner light by continually fueling it with as much wisdom as you can. This can be in the form of educating yourself in both scriptural and practical wisdom. For example, God has been guiding us for millennia about the negative effects of alcohol. Proverbs 23:29-35 vividly depicts the anguish, sorrow, and regret tied to alcohol's trap: it entices with promises of comfort but delivers pain and destruction. Recognizing these truths and pairing them with practical wisdom about how habits form can strengthen your resolve.

Freedom Comes with Focus and Practice

Learning to educate yourself on biblical and worldly temptation can fortify your resolve when it comes to moving on from a substance's hold on your life. Learning to manage temptation (triggers and cravings) through a biblical approach by familiarizing yourself and staying in God's Word can be a major source of power, momentum, and illumination when it comes to finding freedom from life-controlling substances. As a matter of fact, science is just now confirming what God has always told us! You can renew your mind (Romans 12:2) and you can create new neural pathways and methods to navigate your life.

The science of addiction and habit formation reveals how alcohol alters the brain, creating compulsive habits through dopamine-driven rewards. Learning about these changes demystifies the healing process, showing that freedom is not just possible but practical.

Your Life Flows Where Your Thoughts Go

In 2 Corinthians 10:5 (ESV), Paul writes: *"We destroy arguments and every lofty opinion raised against the knowledge of God, and take every thought captive to obey Christ."* By redirecting and taking our thoughts captive—from triggers to gratitude and faith—we form habits aligned with God's will.

As we become more aware of how our thoughts precede our actions, we can get better at redirecting our thoughts. By practicing new habits and spending our time wisely, we will begin to see positive results. In 1 Timothy 4:15 (ESV) Paul reminds us to *"Practice these things, immerse yourself in them, so that all may see your progress."*

You Are Not a Hopeless Case

If one person can succeed at this, then you can. The success of others who decided they were ready will fuel your own progress. 1 Corinthians 10:13 (NLT) states: *"The temptations in your life are no different from what others experience. And God is faithful. He will not allow the temptation to be more than you can stand. When you are tempted, he will show you a way out so that you can endure."*

There's immense value in exploring the personal stories of individuals who've conquered their struggles with alcohol and other substances. Documentaries, podcasts, blogs, and coaching groups provide practical tips and encouragement. Seeing others' success reinforces the truth that freedom is attainable. Consider the Say Goodbye and Imagine podcast, along with others, with stories of transformation and other educational information that will give you hope for something different. In your endeavor, be reminded that God will never give you something more than you can bear.

Heal Your Trauma for Faster Freedom

Trauma, stress, and anxiety often lie at the root of problematic drinking. Research shows a strong connection between childhood trauma, PTSD, and substance abuse. When trauma isn't addressed, it can linger silently, shaping behaviors, influencing relationships, and even impacting one's sense of self and purpose. Unresolved trauma shapes behaviors and influences relationships, often leading to self-medication with substances. Understanding and addressing this trauma through counseling and therapeutic modalities will help your coping mechanisms without substances.

The Bible reminds us of God's healing power in Psalms 147:3 (NLT): *"He heals the brokenhearted and bandages their wounds."* Another encouraging verse is Isaiah 41:10 (NLT): *"Don't be afraid, for I am with you. Don't be discouraged, for I am your God. I will strengthen you and help you. I will hold you up with my victorious right hand."* With God's strength, knowledge and support, you can overcome trauma's hold on your life.

Alcohol Destroys the Temple God Asked Us to Care For

This poison disrupts your connection to the Holy Spirit, and it harms the temple we were instructed to care for. In 1 Corinthians 6:19-20 (NLT) we are told that our bodies are temples of the Holy Spirit, bought at a high price, *"…..so you must honor God with your body."* Honoring God means caring for our physical and spiritual well-being.

The more you dive into learning about the harmful effects of alcohol, the more fuel for your motivation to move on. Alcohol is a toxin that damages your organs, negatively affects your mental health, and impairs your thinking abilities (you make bad decisions that can lead to physical harm or even death). According to *Alcohol Use and Your Health*, excessive drinking is responsible for *one in five deaths* among adults aged 20–49 years.[19]

Understanding that our body is the temple of the Holy Spirit gives us the right motivation to move forward with our desire to be free from the psychological slavery of alcohol.

Healing Begins Immediately

The good news is that healing begins the moment you stop drinking. The body has a remarkable ability to recover, and God's grace allows for spiritual renewal. *"Even after years of heavy alcohol use, the liver has a remarkable regenerative capacity and, following alcohol removal, can recover a significant portion of its original mass and function. Other organs show recovery after abstinence as well."*[20]

As you step away from alcohol, you'll find not only physical restoration but also a renewed relationship with God and a brighter future filled with purpose and light. Every step towards healing begins with your willingness to say, "I'm ready" to embrace the plan God has waiting for you. Unfortunately, the longer you continue to misuse alcohol, the more harm you cause, and the harder it is to repair that damage. Too often, people wait for the unthinkable diagnosis to occur to make a change. Don't let that be you.

Freedom Can Be Yours

I've said it before, and I will say it again: *you are not alone.* Hundreds of millions of people worldwide are on this journey, and with education, determination, and God's help, you, too, can find lasting freedom. Educating yourself about the habit-forming brain and the health impacts of long-term alcohol use provides critical insights into the nature of psychological slavery and how to overcome this state. Learning ways to employ neural reprogramming techniques, such as meditating on God's Word, prayer, and gratitude, helps reshape harmful habits into positive behaviors.

By weaving together spiritual practices, educational resources, and community support, individuals who choose freedom in Christ can find a comprehensive path to healing that nurtures their mental, physical, and spiritual well-being. Freedom from the psychological slavery of alcohol can be yours. It begins with the bold decision to say, "I'm ready," and to take the first step in faith toward the promising life God has planned for you.

With all of the puzzle pieces accessed, consider yourself *Prepared to Quit*! If you haven't done the exercises related to each chapter, download the workbook by following the QR Code below:

Prepare to Quit Workbook

If This Book Helped You…

We hope *Prepare to Quit* has been a meaningful step on your journey toward a Spirit-filled life beyond alcohol. If the keys and reflections in these pages have inspired or empowered you, would you consider sharing your experience?

Here's How You Can Help Others Find Freedom:

1. **Leave a Review**
   Reviews on Amazon, Goodreads, or wherever you purchased this book are some of the best ways to help others discover it.

2. **Spread the Word**
   Tell a friend, family member, or someone in your community about this book.

3. **Stay Connected**
   Scan the QR Code below to follow us on social media and stay connected

Rose Ann Forte

NOTES

1. See https://www.niaaa.nih.gov/alcohols-effects-health/alcohol-topics/alcohol-facts-and-statistics/alcohol-use-disorder-aud-united-states-age-groups-and-demographic-characteristics.
2. See https://www.gpb.org/news/2025/01/03/new-study-sheds-light-on-americas-biggest-drug-problem-alcohol.
3. See https://www.niaaa.nih.gov/alcohols-effects-health/alcohol-topics-z/alcohol-facts-and-statistics/alcohol-treatment-united-states.
4. See https://www.who.int/news-room/fact-sheets/detail/alcohol.
5. See https://arcr.niaaa.nih.gov/volume/42/1/niaaa-50th-anniversary-festschrift-editor.
6. See https://www.hopkinsmedicine.org/health/wellness-and-prevention/alcohol-and-heart-health-separating-fact-from-fiction.
7. See https://www.mentalhealth.org.uk/explore-mental-health/a-z-topics/alcohol-and-mental-health.
8. See https://www.niaaa.nih.gov.
9. See https://pmc.ncbi.nlm.nih.gov/articles/PMC6438088.
10. See https://www.gatewayfoundation.org/blog/drinking-speeds-up-aging.
11. See https://www.cdc.gov/mmwr/volumes/73/wr/mm7308a1.htm?s_cid=mm7308a1_w.
12. See https://www.hhs.gov/about/news/2025/01/03/us-surgeon-general-issues-new-advisory-link-alcohol-cancer-risk.html.
13. See https://pmc.ncbi.nlm.nih.gov/articles/PMC6876499.
14. See https://www.cnn.com/2022/01/22/health/pandemic-drinking-problem-wellness/index.html.
15. See https://www.forbes.com/councils/forbescoachescouncil/2020/01/08/why-you-should-invest-in-yourself.
16. See https://www.nextgen-wealth.com/blog/the-top-5-benefits-to-investing-in-yourself.

17. See https://www.amazon.com/12-Rules-for-Life-audiobook/dp/B0797Y87JC.
18. See https://pmc.ncbi.nlm.nih.gov/articles/PMC6759672.
19. See https://www.cdc.gov/alcohol/about-alcohol-use/index.html.
20. See https://pmc.ncbi.nlm.nih.gov/articles/PMC8041137.

About the Author

Rose Ann Forte is a faith-driven leader, coach, course creator and best-selling author dedicated to helping individuals break free from the psychological slavery of alcohol and other life-interfering behaviors. A former C-Suite executive and ministry leader, Rose Ann balanced a thriving career with raising four children, all while maintaining what she believed was a manageable social drinking habit. However, as life's pressures mounted—through career demands, a difficult marriage, and personal struggles—her alcohol use escalated, leading to deep emotional and spiritual unrest.

Feeling disconnected from God and seeking true transformation, Rose Ann embarked on a journey that would forever change her life. In 2020, during the COVID-19 pandemic, she enrolled in a coaching program to put alcohol aside for three months. That experience was not only life-changing but also spiritually renewing. She recognized how God's wisdom was woven into the process of renewing her mind and transforming her heart. Through this, she developed a powerful approach that merges biblical truths with scientific insights on habit formation, empowering others to shift their mindset from "I can't do it" to "I get to"

Her passion for helping others led her to write *The Plans He Has for Me*, a daily devotional that supports individuals seeking faith-filled transformation. She later co-authored *Transformed by His Promises* with Dr. Karl Benzio, the Medical Director of the American Association of

Christian Counselors, expanding on biblical principles to help people overcome life-interfering behaviors.

Her latest book, *Prepare to Quit*, is designed for those considering a break from alcohol or struggling with their relationship with drinking. It offers a faith-centered approach to navigating this journey, emphasizing biblical wisdom, neuroscience, and the power of mindset shifts. Whether someone is engaging in personal reflection, working through a faith-based recovery program, or seeking additional support, *Prepare to Quit* provides practical and spiritual tools to help individuals move forward with confidence and hope.

Rose Ann also hosts the podcast Say Goodbye and Imagine!, where she interviews experts and individuals who have experienced profound personal growth and healing through faith-based recovery.

When she's not writing or coaching, Rose Ann enjoys spending time with her four adult children, exploring the beauty of Phoenix, and serving in her local church community. She believes that no matter how deep the struggle, God will always be available to shine a light on a pathway out. Freedom is possible for anyone willing to take the first step.